Keep Abortion Safe & Legal

This book wouldn't exist without the help of the special people at NARAL. Thanks to Ann McGuinness, Kate Michelman, Jill Spector and Karen Paul.

This book is dedicated to every woman who has ever agonized over the choice to have an abortion, and to her right to make that decision in private.

The Postcard Activist™ series includes:
Keep Abortion Safe & Legal
Ban Censorship
No Handguns

ISBN 1-879096-00-5 10 9 8 7 6 5 4 3 2 1

Distributed to the trade by Publishers Group West. **Call 800 365-3453 for orders.**
Published by The Postcard Activist, Box 660, Yonkers, NY 10710

PRINTED IN THE USA ON RECYCLED PAPER

FOREWORD

Recent events — most notably the U.S. Supreme Court's 1989 *Webster* decision — shocked Americans and energized a previously complacent pro-choice majority. *Webster* gave state legislators the power to restrict abortion rights, revolutionizing American politics and starting a new chapter in the fight for the freedom to choose.

With the increasingly important role abortion is playing in elections at every level of government, it is critical to let our public officials know that the intensely personal decisions about abortion belong to women and their families and **not** to politicians.

Twenty years ago, before the decision in *Roe v. Wade*, abortion was illegal in the United States. Few of us can remember that time without shuddering. If you weren't affluent enough to travel to where a safe abortion was available, terminating an unwanted pregnancy meant shame, degradation and the risk of back-alley butchery. Botched abortions were common. Many women were maimed. Many women died.

A few hundred dedicated women and men formed the National Abortion Rights Action League (NARAL) in 1969 to end this tragedy. From the very beginning, NARAL — the grassroots political arm of the pro-choice movement — faced an uphill battle against forces determined to take away our rights. In fact, we were given little chance of succeeding in those days.

This period in NARAL history culminated in the most important single event in the history of the pro-choice movement: The Supreme Court's landmark *Roe v. Wade* decision in 1973 that finally legalized abortion.

Some NARAL activists and supporters thought that *Roe* signified the end of our battle. They were wrong. In reality, the battle had just begun...

Since *Roe*, thousands of bills have been introduced to restrict the right to choose — in Congress and in statehouses. After the *Webster* decision, this activity intensified. In almost every state in the country, restrictive legislation was introduced. Bills have even been introduced that would prohibit abortion in *all* cases — including victims of rape and incest. We fight hard to protect our fundamental rights, and we have been successful in defeating many potentially dangerous bills. But it only takes one bill passed by one legislature to overturn *Roe* and take away our right to choose.

Today, NARAL is close to half a million members strong. But that is not enough. Anti–choice forces are formidable. They are well-funded and they have been organized for eighteen years.

Pro-choice Americans must use the political process to prevent politicians from making our most personal decisions. Too often, we take our personal rights for granted until they are critically threatened.

We must all raise our voices. We need your help now. We need your support, your dollars, and most of all, your letters. Democracy works in this country, but only if we make it work.

Buy this book. Buy another copy for a friend. And send the 30 postcards. Please. Do it now, before it's too late.

Let your lawmakers know that in America, it is the people, not the politicians, who decide.

Kate Michelman
Executive Director
National Abortion Rights Action League.

HOW TO USE THIS BOOK

Is a postcard *really* going to make a difference?

Legislators and corporations are quick to respond to their constituents. And the easiest way to tell them what you're thinking is to send a postcard.

If you follow a few simple steps, you can maximize the chance that your postcard will be read and acted upon.

1. *Be sure that the address is complete.* Many of the postcards in this book are addressed to local politicians. You need to fill in the correct names and addresses. The easiest way to do this is to call your local League of Women Voters (they have more than 1,000 offices around the country). They're listed in the phone book under *League*.

2. *Add your personal comments.* Each postcard has room on the bottom for you to express yourself. Threats are probably not effective. Instead, personalize the issue by writing about how it affects you and your family.

3. *Add your name and address.* ou may even get a response. Remember, anonymous letters don't get counted.

4. *Don't forget to add a stamp.* The post office won't deliver without one.

Do it now. Before it's too late...

Governor

Since the Supreme Court's decision in *Webster*, the most crucial abortion rights battles will be held at the state level. A veto by the governor can mean the difference.

This postcard to your governor is perhaps the most important one in the entire book.

Dear Governor:

As a voter, I'm very concerned about the abortion rights issue. A woman's right to choose is a private one, and must not be taken away by any state or by Congress.

Please keep abortion safe and legal.

Name ______________________
Address ___________________
City, State Zip ________________
Phone ________________

The Honorable ________________
Governor
The State House

___________ _____ _____

Governor

Contact your local League of Woman Voters for the correct name and address.

TO:

____

Governor

Date Sent:

____

Senate

The Senate makes crucial decisions regarding the legal right to choose and confirms nominees to the Supreme Court.

The two Senators from your state will be particularly responsive to a message from one of their constituents.

Dear Senator:

I'm pro-choice and I vote.

As one of your constituents, I'm writing to ask you to support the Freedom of Choice Act to keep abortion safe and legal and to oppose any Supreme Court nominee does not recognize the constitutionally protected right to privacy, which includes the right to choose.

Name ______________________
Address ___________________
City, State Zip ______________
Phone _______________

The Honorable ________________
U.S. Senate
Washington, DC 20510

Senate

Contact your local League of Woman Voters for the correct name and address.

TO:

____

U.S. Senate

Date Sent:

____

Senate

The Senate makes crucial decisions regarding the legal right to choose and confirms nominees to the Supreme Court.

The two Senators from your state will be particularly responsive to a message from one of their constituents.

Dear Senator:

I'm pro-choice and I vote.

As one of your constituents, I'm writing to ask you to support the Freedom of Choice Act to keep abortion safe and legal and to oppose any Supreme Court nominee does not recognize the constitutionally protected right to privacy, which includes the right to choose.

Name ____________________
Address __________________
City, State Zip ______________
Phone _______________

The Honorable ________________
U.S. Senate
Washington, DC 20510

Senate

Contact your local League of Woman Voters for the correct name and address.

TO:

____

U.S. Senate

Date Sent:

____

Congress

Crucial funding decisions regarding women's reproductive choice are made in Congress—decisions that affect clinics, health programs and even the legal right to choose.

Your U.S. Representative will be very sensitive to views expressed by his or her constituents.

Dear Congressman:

I'm pro-choice and I vote.

As one of your constituents, I'm writing to ask you to support the Freedom of Choice Act to keep abortion safe and legal. A woman's right to choose is a private one, and it must not be taken away by any state or by Congress.

Name ______________________
Address ____________________
City, State Zip _______________
Phone _______________

The Honorable ________________
U.S. Representative
Washington, DC 20515

Congress

Contact your local League of Woman Voters for the correct name and address.

TO:

____

U.S. Representative

Date Sent:

____

Surgeon

The Surgeon General is the government's leading specialist on health.

The anti-choice crusade against abortion creates an enormous health risk, especially among women too poor to travel out of state.

Dear Dr. Novella:

Freedom of choice is a public health issue. When abortion is safe and legal, women are healthier.

Please do everything in your power to ensure a woman's right to choose a safe and legal abortion.

Name ______________________

Address ____________________

City, State Zip ______________

Phone _______________

Dr. Antonia Novella
The Surgeon General
Department of H&HS
200 Independence Ave. SW
Washington, DC 20201

Surgeon

TO:

Antonia
Novella

Department of H&HS

Date Sent:

President

As the most visible elected official in the country, George Bush sets the tone for all national policy.

He also has the crucial role of nominating Justices to the Supreme Court, a vital battle-ground in the fight for choice.

Dear President Bush:

I'm pro-choice and I vote.

The majority of voters in this country support a woman's fundamental right to choose. I'm asking you to respect this right in your policies and in your nominations to the Supreme Court. Please work to ensure a woman's right to choose a safe and legal abortion.

Name ____________________
Address ____________________
City, State Zip ____________________
Phone ____________________

The Honorable George Bush
President of the United States
The White House
1400 Pennsylvania Ave.
Washington, DC 20500

President

TO:

George
Bush

The White House

Date Sent:

____

Atty Gen'l

As the nation's most senior law enforcement official, the Attorney General determines the tone and level of prosecution and enforcement of many abortion-related laws. It is vitally important that the Attorney General respects our right to choice.

Dear Attorney General Thornburgh:

Abortion is not, and should never be, a crime. Bombing abortion clinics, however, is terrorism.

Please work to preserve our rights, and urge the courts to uphold our fundamental right to choose.

Name ______________________

Address ____________________

City, State Zip ________________

Phone ________________

Richard Thornburgh
Attorney General
Department of Justice
Constitution Ave. & 10 Street NW
Washington, DC 20530

Atty Gen'l

TO:

Richard
Thornburgh

Department of Justice

Date Sent:

VP

As the tie breaking vote in the Senate, the Vice President may someday cast a crucial ballot on the right to choose.

In the interim, he often represents the interests of anti-choice activists, and he needs to know how the majority feel about the right to choose.

Dear Vice President Quayle:

I'm pro-choice and I vote.

The majority of Americans support a woman's right to choose whether or not to have an abortion. I urge you to work to keep abortion safe and legal.

Name ____________________
Address __________________
City, State Zip _______________
Phone ______________

VP

The Honorable Dan Quayle
Vice President of the United States
c/o The Senate
The Capitol
Washington, DC 20510

TO:

Dan
Quayle

c/o The Senate

Date Sent:

Speaker

As Speaker of the House, Tom Foley exercises a great deal of influence over the work of Congress and determines whether and when a bill will be considered on the floor of the House.

Dear Mr. Speaker:

I'm pro-choice and I vote.

Please represent the interests of the majority of voters in this country and work to pass the Freedom of Choice Act. A woman's right to choose is a private one, and must not be taken away by any state or by Congress.

Name ______________________
Address ____________________
City, State Zip ______________
Phone ________________

The Honorable Thomas Foley
Speaker of the House
House of Representatives
Washington, DC 20510

Speaker

TO:

Thomas
Foley

House of
Representatives

Date Sent:

____

Senate

The Senate approves the appointment of every federal judge, including those on the Supreme Court.

In addition, the Majority Leader determines whether and when any piece of legislation will be considered by the Senate.

Dear Senator Mitchell:

I'm pro-choice and I vote.

Please do not allow the President to pack the Supreme Court with Justices who don't recognize the Constitutional protection for the right to privacy and the right to choose. The U.S. Senate should represent the interests of the majority of voters in this country by assuring passage of the Freedom of Choice Act.

Name ____________________
Address ____________________
City, State Zip ____________________
Phone ____________________

The Honorable George Mitchell
Senate Majority Leader
U. S. Senate
Washington, DC 20510

Senate

TO:

George
Mitchell

U. S. Senate

Date Sent:

Approp.

The Appropriations Committee controls the billions of dollars spent by the U.S. each year. This includes money for health programs, here and abroad.

Dear Mr. Chairman:

I'm pro-choice and I vote.

The majority of voters agree that a woman's right to choose is a private one, and must not be taken away by any state or by Congress. As Senate Appropriations Chair, please do everything you can to ensure a woman's right to choose a safe and legal abortion.

Name ______________________
Address ___________________
City, State Zip _______________
Phone _______________

The Honorable Robert Byrd
Chair, Appropriations Committee
U. S. Senate
Washington, DC 20510

Approp.

TO:

Robert
Byrd

U. S. Senate

Date Sent:

Approp.

The Appropriations Committee controls billions of dollars spent by the U.S. each year. This includes money for health programs, here and abroad.

Dear Chairman Whitten:

I'm pro-choice and I vote.

The majority of voters agree that a woman's right to choose is a private one, and must not be taken away by any state or by Congress. As House Appropriations Chair, please do everything you can to ensure a woman's right to choose a safe and legal abortion by seeking passage of the Reproductive Health Equity Act.

Name ____________________

Address __________________

City, State Zip ______________

Phone ______________

The Honorable Jamie Whitten
Chair, Appropriations Committee
U. S. House of Representatives
Washington, DC 20515

Approp.

TO:

Jamie
Whitten

U. S. House of
Representatives

Date Sent:

____

Approp.

The Senate Labor, Health and Human Services and Education Appropriations Subcommittee draws up the bills that determine how the many billions of dollars allocated for health programs will be spent in this country.

Dear Mr. Chairman:

I'm pro-choice and I vote.

The majority of voters agree that a woman's right to choose is a private one, and must not be taken away by any state or by Congress. Please do everything you can to ensure a woman's right to choose a safe and legal abortion by seeking passage of the Reproductive Health Equity act.

Name ____________________
Address ____________________
City, State Zip ____________________
Phone ____________________

The Honorable Tom Harkin
Chairman
HHS & Education Approp. Subcommittee
U.S. Senate
Washington, DC 20510

Approp.

TO:

Tom
Harkin

HHS & Education
Approp. Subcommitte

Date Sent:

Health

The House Labor, Health and Human Services and Education Appropriations Subcommittee draws up the bills that determine how the many billions of dollars allocated for health programs will be spent.

Dear Mr. Chairman:

I'm pro-choice and I vote.

The majority of voters agree that a woman's right to choose is a private one, and must not be taken away by any state or by Congress. Please do everything you can ensure a woman's right to choose a safe and legal abortion.

Name ______________________

Address ___________________

City, State Zip _______________

Phone ________________

The Honorable William H. Natcher
Chairman
HHS & Education Appropriations
Subcommittee
Washington, DC 20515

Health

TO:

William H.
Natcher

HHS & Education
Appropriations

Date Sent:

Senate

The Senate Majority Whip is highly influential in determining the outcome of legislation in the Senate.

Dear Senator Ford:

I'm pro-choice and I vote.

The majority of voters agree that a woman's right to choose is a private one, and must not be taken away by any state or by Congress. Please do everything you can to ensure a woman's right to choose a safe and legal abortion by supporting Senate passage of the Freedom of Choice Act.

Name ______________________
Address ____________________
City, State Zip ______________
Phone _______________

The Honorable Wendell Ford
Senate Majority Whip
U. S. Senate
Washington, DC 20510

Senate

TO:

Wendell
Ford

U. S. Senate

Date Sent:

____

Rules

The House Rules Committee determines the order and substance of amendments to most legislation considered by the House.

Dear Mr. Chairman:

I'm pro-choice and I vote.

The majority of voters agree that a woman's right to choose is a private one, and must not be taken away by any state or by Congress. Please do everything you can to ensure a woman's right to choose a safe and legal abortion by supporting House passage of the Freedom of Choice Act.

Name ____________________
Address ____________________
City, State Zip ____________________
Phone ________________

The Honorable Joe Moakley
Chair, House Rules Committee
U.S. House of Representatives
Washington, DC 20515

Rules

TO:

Joe
Moakley

U.S. House of
Representatives

Date Sent:

____

Judiciary

The Senate Judiciary Committee confirms all Federal judges, including those nominated for the Supreme Court.

It is vitally important that the Court represent the interests of *all* Americans, not just the far right.

Dear Mr. Chairman:

I'm pro-choice and I vote.

Please do everything you can to ensure a woman's right to choose a safe and legal abortion by supporting the Fredom of Choice Act and by opposing Supreme Court nominees who do not recognize the Constitutionally protected right to privacy, which includes the right to choose.

Name ______________________
Address ____________________
City, State Zip ________________
Phone _______________

The Honorable Joseph Biden
Senate Judiciary Committee Chair
U. S. Senate
Washington, DC 20510

Judiciary

TO:

Joseph
Biden

U. S. Senate

Date Sent:

____

Judiciary

The House Judiciary Committee considers constitutional amendments (as well as other important legislation) affecting the right to choose .

Among the crucial pieces of legislation it will consider is the Freedom of Choice Act.

Dear Mr. Chairman:

I'm pro-choice and I vote.

Please do everything you can to ensure a woman's right to choose a safe and legal abortion. The House Judiciary Committee should work to assure passage of the Freedom of Choice Act.

Name ____________________

Address __________________

City, State Zip ______________

Phone ______________

Judiciary

The Honorable Jack Brooks
Chair, House Judiciary Committee
U.S. House of Representatives
Washington, DC 20515

TO:

Jack
Brooks

U.S. House of
Representatives

Date Sent:

GOP

The Republican National Committee develops strategy and message for the Republican Party. The Committee helps formulate the party platform and choose presidential nominees.

(SEND THIS CARD IF YOU'RE A REPUBLICAN)

Dear Mr. Chairman:

I'm a Republican, I'm pro-choice and I vote.

Please do everything you can to keep abortion safe, legal and accessible to those who choose it. For the Republican party to truly reflect the views of its constituency, it must include a plank in its platform that acknowledges support for the right to choose.

Name ________________________

Address ______________________

City, State Zip ________________

Phone _________________

Clayton Yeutter
Chairman
Republican National Committee
310 First Street SE
Washington, DC 20003

GOP

TO:

Clayton
Yeutter

Republican National
Committee

Date Sent:

____

DNC

The Democratic National Committee develops strategy and message for the Democratic Party. The Committee helps formulate the party platform and choose presidential nominees.

(SEND THIS CARD IF YOU'RE A DEMOCRAT)

Dear Mr. Chairman:

I'm a Democrat, I'm pro-choice and I vote.

Please do everything you can to keep abortion safe, legal and accessible to those who choose it. For the Democratic party to reflect the views of its constituency, it must continue to aggressively include a plank in its platform that enthusiastically affirms support for the right to choose.

Name ____________________
Address __________________
City, State Zip ______________
Phone ______________

DNC

Ronald Brown
Chairman
Democratic National Committee
430 South Capitol St. SE
Washington, DC 20003

TO:

Ronald
Brown

Democratic National
Committee

Date Sent:

FDA

The FDA is responsible for approving all medications that are sold in this country. Contraceptives that are safer and more convenient are being developed, and the FDA should not allow politics to interfere with the approval process.

Dear Commissioner Kessler:

I'm pro-choice and I vote.

The new drug RU 486 represents a technical breakthrough for women seeking a safe alternative to surgical abortion. It has been proven in France, and I urge you to conduct further tests and then allow its sale in this country.

Please move swiftly on other new contraceptive methods, drugs and treatments that will increase the safety for women choosing abortion.

Name ________________________
Address ______________________
City, State Zip __________________
Phone _________________

Dr. David Kessler
Acting Commissioner
Food & Drug Administration
5600 Fishers Lane
Rockville, MD 20857

FDA

TO:

David
Kessler

Food & Drug
Administration

Date Sent:

NIH

The NIH is one of the most important medical research organizations in the country. By focusing increased resources on the new and improved methods of contraceptive care, the NIH can increase the health and well being of millions of women.

Dear Director Raub:

Millions of American women are faced with daily choices about contraception, pregnancy, abortion and fertility.

Please focus more of your research efforts on these crucial issues. By allowing women safer, easier ways to make a reproductive choice, the NIH will benefit all of us.

Name ______________________
Address ___________________
City, State Zip ________________
Phone _______________

NIH

Dr. William Raub
Director
National Institutes of Health
Building One, 9000 Rockville Pike
Bethesda, MD 20892

TO:

William
Raub

National Institutes o
Health

Date Sent:

Michigan

Michigan is a crucial flip state in the battle over choice. Recently elected Governor Engler ran on an anti-choice platform, and would sign legislation to severely restrict or outlaw abortion.

Our message to the Governor is urgent.

Dear Governor Engler:

The freedom of choice is *not* just a local issue. It is about the fundamental right of a woman to choose.

The women of Michigan **must** have the right to decide what is best for them and their families. Please protect the right to choose.

Name ________________________
Address ______________________
City, State Zip __________________
Phone _________________

Michigan

The Honorable John Engler
Governor
Capitol
Box 30013
Lansing, MI 48909

TO:

John
Engler

Capitol

Date Sent:

____

Missouri

Missouri, the home state of the infamous *Webster* decision, will continue to be a battleground state.

Both houses of the legislature and the Governor oppose abortion as a legal option.

Dear Governor Ashcroft:

The freedom of choice is *not* just a local issue. It is about the fundamental right of a woman to choose.

The women of Missouri **must** have the right to choose what is best for them and their families. Please protect the right to choose.

Name ____________________
Address ____________________
City, State Zip ____________________
Phone ________________

The Honorable John Ashcroft
Governor
Capitol, Box 720
Jefferson, MO 65102

Missouri

TO:

John
Ashcroft

Governor

Date Sent:

Minn.

The Minnesota Legislature has already demonstrated its receptiveness to imposing dangerous restrictions on the right to choose.

We need the Governor's veto to block further attempts to chip away at this right.

Dear Governor Carlson:

The freedom of choice is *not* just a local issue. It is about the fundamental right of a woman to choose.

The women of Minnesota **must** have the right to decide what is best for them and their families. Please protect the right to choose.

Name ____________________

Address ____________________

City, State Zip ____________________

Phone ____________________

Minn.

The Honorable Arne Carlson
Governor
130 State Capitol
St. Paul, MN 55155

TO:

Arne
Carlson

Governor

Date Sent:

Louisiana

Louisiana is a crucial state in the abortion debate. Governor Roemer vetoed the most restrictive abortion law in the country— one that banned choice even for victims of rape and incest.

Similar bills are expected this year. He is up for re-election in 1991.

Dear Governor Roemer:

The freedom of choice is *not* just a local issue. It is about the fundamental right of a woman to choose. Thank you for your support last year.

I'm pro-choice, and I vote. The women of Louisiana **must** have the right to choose what is best for them and their families. If your legislature is successful in outlawing abortion, innocent women will die.

Name ______________________
Address ____________________
City, State Zip ________________
Phone ________________

Louisiana

The Honorable Buddy Roemer
Governor
State House
PO Box 94004
Baton Rouge, LA 70804

TO:

Buddy
Roemer

State House

Date Sent:

Alabama

Alabama is a crucial state in the abortion debate for the next several years. Governor Hunt is anti-choice, and could sign legislation to severely restrict or outlaw abortion.

Governor Hunt needs to hear our message.

Dear Governor Hunt:

The freedom of choice is *not* just a local issue. It is about the fundamental right of a woman to choose.

The women of Alabama **must** have the right to choose what is best for them and their families. Please protect the right to choose.

Name ______________________

Address ____________________

City, State Zip ________________

Phone _______________

Alabama

The Honorable Guy Hunt
Governor
11 South Union Street, Second Floor
Montgomery, AL 36130

TO:

Guy
Hunt

Governor

Date Sent:

Kansas

Kansas is a crucial state in the abortion debate for the next several years. Governor Finney ran on an anti-choice platform, and could sign legislation to severely restrict or outlaw abortion.

Our message to the Governor is urgent.

Dear Governor Finney:

The freedom of choice is *not* just a local issue. It is about the fundamental right of a woman to choose.

The women of Kansas **must** have the right to choose what is best for them and their families. Please protect the right to choose.

Name ____________________
Address __________________
City, State Zip ______________
Phone ______________

The Honorable Joan Finney
Governor
Second Floor, State Capitol
Topeka, KS 66612

Kansas

TO:

Joan
Finney

Governor

Date Sent:

____

H&HS

As head of the department responsible for implementing family planning measures, the Health & Human Services Secretary has the power to make a real difference in the lives of millions of women.

Dear Secretary Sullivan:

The Department of Health & Human Services needs to make family planning and counseling services a priority. Please work to ensure a woman's right to choose a safe and legal abortion.

Name ____________________

Address ____________________

City, State Zip ____________________

Phone ____________________

H&HS

The Honorable Louis Sullivan
Secretary
Department of Health & Human Services
200 Independence Ave. SW
Washington, DC 20201

TO:

Louis
Sullivan

Department of Health
& Human Services

Date Sent:

Solicitor

The Solicitor General argues cases before the Supreme Court, both when the United States is the plaintiff and in other relevant cases.

The Solicitor General plays an important role in influencing the Court.

Dear Solicitor General Starr:

Abortion is not a crime. Every woman must have the right to choose.

Americans believe that the Supreme Court ruled properly in *Roe v. Wade*. Therefore, the government should cease seeking venues in which to overrule *Roe* and make abortion a crime.

Name ____________________
Address __________________
City, State Zip ______________
Phone ______________

Solicitor

Kenneth Starr
Solicitor General
U.S. Department of Justice
10th and Constitution Ave. NW
Washington, DC 20530

TO:

Kenneth
Starr

U.S. Department of Justice

Date Sent:

____

Ohio

Ohio is a crucial state in the abortion debate. Recently elected Governor Voinovich ran on an anti-choice platform, and could sign legislation to severely restrict or outlaw abortion.

Our message to the Governor is urgent.

Dear Governor Voinovich:

The freedom of choice is *not* just a local issue. It is about the fundamental right of a woman to choose.

The women of Ohio **must** have the right to decide what is best for them and their families. Please protect the right to choose.

Name ______________________
Address ____________________
City, State Zip ________________
Phone _______________

Ohio

The Honorable George Voinovich
Governor
77 South High Street, 30th Floor
Columbus, OH 43215

TO:

George
Voinovich

Governor

Date Sent:

Friend

Help spread the word! Send this card to a friend, and you can double the impact of our efforts.

The more cards we send, the more likely it is that the people in charge will represent the views of the majority—our views. Send this card to a friend who cares.

Dear Friend:

Please go out and buy a copy of *Keep Abortion Safe & Legal.* The book is filled with postcards that let us tell politicians exactly how we feel on this vital issue.

Buy the book and send the cards. Together, we can make a difference.

Name ______________________
Address ____________________
City, State Zip ________________
Phone ________________

Friend

TO:

Date Sent:

Friend

Help spread the word! Send this card to a friend, and you can double the impact of our efforts.

The more cards we send, the more likely it is that the people in charge will represent the views of the majority—our views. Send this card to a friend who cares.

Dear Friend:

Please go out and buy a copy of *Keep Abortion Safe & Legal*. The book is filled with postcards that let us tell politicians exactly how we feel on this vital issue.

Buy the book and send the cards. Together, we can make a difference.

Name ______________________
Address ____________________
City, State Zip ________________
Phone ________________

Friend

TO:

Date Sent:

Friend

Help spread the word! Send this card to a friend, and you can double the impact of our efforts.

The more cards we send, the more likely it is that the people in charge will represent the views of the majority—our views. Send this card to a friend who cares.

Dear Friend:

Please go out and buy a copy of *Keep Abortion Safe & Legal.* The book is filled with postcards that let us tell politicians exactly how we feel on this vital issue.

Buy the book and send the cards. Together, we can make a difference.

Name ______________________
Address ___________________
City, State Zip _______________
Phone ________________

Friend

TO:

Date Sent:

NARAL

NARAL has been fighting for the right to choose for more than 20 years. With more than 450,000 members throughout the country, NARAL speaks for the silent majority. They need your membership.

Do it now. Before it's too late.

Dear NARAL:

Yes, I want to join NARAL to protect our right to choose.

I would like to become the newest NARAL member. Enclosed is my check for:

❒ $25 ❒ $35 ❒ $50 ❒ $100 ❒ other $_____

(Because of the hard-hitting political activities of NARAL, contributions are not tax deductible. Corporate contributions cannot be accepted.)

Name ____________________

Address ____________________

City, State Zip ____________________

Phone ____________________

Membership Department
NARAL
1101 14th Street NW
Washington, DC 20005

NARAL

TO:

NARAL

Date Sent: